THE ART OF ALCHEMY

Inner Alchemy & the Revelation of the Philosopher's Stone

Gabriyell Sarom

Contents

Publications

The Art of Mysticism

The Step-by-step practical guide to Mysticism & Spiritual Meditations

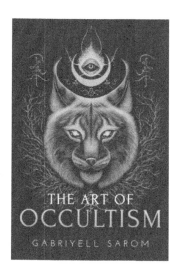

The Art of Occultism

The Secrets of High Occultism & Inner Exploration

The Art of Magick

The Mystery of Deep Magick &
Divine Rituals

**Subscribe to Gabriyell Sarom's
Newsletter and receive the book:**

*Divine Abilities:
3 Techniques to Awaken Divine Abilities*

www.sacredmystery.org

Introduction

From the dawn of humanity to the modern age, alchemy has always been a subject of great curiosity. Its mere mention brings old tales of wiseman working in smoke-filled alchemical laboratories trying to transform metals into gold whilst creating elixirs that immortalized the body.

While this mythical picture is still prevalent today, alchemy is a field of inquiry whose ultimate quest is spiritual emancipation. The process of transmutation, whereby the base metal of our earthly existence is rearranged by fire into the dazzling gold that signifies Spirit and truth at its highest level, has captivated an unbroken line of genuine seekers since ancient times.

Although it may appear to be an arcane discipline filled with cryptic and often unintelligible language, alchemy holds a powerful treasure once its lexicon and teachings are decoded. Because of its esoteric nature, being shrouded in riddles and secrecy, it is easy to become trapped in a maze of apparent nonsense. Don't expect to find that same approach and teachings here.

This book is centered on practices and procedures of Inner Alchemy, and it aims to shed new light on this ancient tradition, revealing its power to deeply transmute our body, energy, mind, and soul. It streamlines the entire path and bypasses all of the obscurity inherent in alchemy, making it functional and approachable.

Inner Alchemy is not about creating medicines or heating toxic materials in brick furnaces to create bizarre compounds, but about using our body and mind as the alchemical laboratory.

At diverse points in time, there has been an alchemist, book, or teaching that encourages students to embark on the fascinating journey of alchemical exploration and motivates them to reach the unfathomable ends of human potential.

We sincerely hope the reader enjoys this work and that it may serve as that inspirational lodestar towards the much-coveted Philosopher's Stone.

SECTION 1

The Apprenticeship

$$1$$

Awakening to Alchemy

My first real-world adventure into alchemy came when an acquaintance of a friend named Mesmer was giving a lecture about chemistry and invited me to attend. To be honest, I had no particular interest in chemistry. Nevertheless, I attended that evening and sat through about half an hour of his presentation, and something about it held my attention and convinced me to stay for the rest of his talk. This wasn't the standard chemistry that I was expecting, but what someone could call "mystical chemistry" or "chemistry of the spirit", which I'd later call Spiritual or Inner Alchemy.

When the presentation ended, Mesmer invited anyone

from the audience who had a question to go ahead and ask it. Strangely enough, nobody asked him anything. "They're mostly passersby", I thought to myself.

Mystical subjects have always fascinated me, and alchemy is no exception. It's the stuff spiritual legends are made of. That lecture further sparked my curiosity, and I felt that I couldn't leave without asking him what he *really* knew about alchemy.

When people began to leave the room, I walked towards him and asked precisely that. He paused for a long minute, looking at me as if he didn't want to answer my question. "Come to my house next Monday at 6 p.m.", he said eventually.

I showed up at 6 p.m. on Monday at Mesmer's house, and as soon as I walked in through the door, Mesmer shut it behind me and locked it! Then, he put a blindfold over my eyes so I couldn't see where I was going, grabbed my arm firmly, and led me into a secret room in his house.

After entering this mysterious room and closing the door behind us, Mesmer took off my blindfold. We were in a medium-sized room with three meditation cushions, a couple of mats, and an altar with candles and various mystical symbols and figures. I also saw a small shelf with a glass sphere with a long neck, multiple cylinders, vials, bottles, flasks, and transparent jars filled with colorful powders and liquids. The scent of incense hung in the air.

This room had a distinct ambiance; it exuded mysticism in every corner. It was the first time I saw a *laboratorium*.

"Sit down", said Mesmer gently. "Alchemy is not what people think it is. It is not about turning lead into gold". He then expanded on what he had already presented in his lecture, describing how alchemy works and the types of basic procedures that one could perform.

I was much younger than Mesmer, so I took the apprentice role. Notwithstanding my youth, I already had solid experience with mystical teachings and practices. This meant that I could easily absorb his teachings and comprehend how to use them in my own life and mystical pilgrimage. Because Mesmer was so gifted and had such a profound understanding of the human body and soul, it wasn't that difficult to incorporate his teachings into my own.

Throughout this time, I received extensive alchemical training, learning various alchemical and mystical teachings, processes, and techniques with the goal of awakening the real alchemical process within myself: transmuting my stone-ego into the divine gold.

This is also the purpose of this presentation: teaching the reader how to use this exquisite art to achieve the most beautiful alchemical process in the universe.

2

What is Alchemy?

Alchemy is a vibrant word. Its mere mention brings old tales of wisemen working in their secret chambers. It has always been a subject of great curiosity, but in present times, it has been relegated to the domain of myths and legends.

Alchemy may be shrouded in esoteric mysteries, but its meaning is unambiguous: it is the art of transformation. Alchemy is a mystical discipline that allows anyone to transform something into a better, higher version of itself.

Alchemists seek transformation in all levels of reality: material, energetic, mental, and spiritual. Whether it is a physical object such as a metal or your body, or a non-physical object such as emotions, vital force, or the mind, alchemy provides the creative process and medium by which a higher degree of transformation can occur.

There are many theories from where alchemy may have originated. Some say that otherworldly beings brought this knowledge from the firmament above, while others point to a meditating monk or priest who found this ancient mystical treasure while in deep meditation thousands of years ago. However, the truth about how it really came into our world is lost in history. Nevertheless, we can trace this esoteric discipline back to the great mysteries of ancient Egypt.

The Egyptian god Toth is usually depicted as the father of alchemy, and many believe he is a divine being. In contrast, others affirm that he was a real person, the "connector" between the divine and human worlds. To the Greeks, he was Hermes, inventor of all sciences and magick. To the Romans, he was Mercury, often portrayed holding the caduceus in his left hand. Like numerous mystical traditions, alchemy is founded on a cocktail of myth and reality.

The word *alchemy* comes from the Greek *khemia*, which was the name the Greeks gave to ancient Egypt, and it means "the land of black earth" (derived from fertile black soil caused by the Nile's yearly flood). This was because alchemy was "imported" to Greece from Egypt. It was only later that the Arabic prefix *Al* ("the") was added, forming *Alkimiya*, which ultimately means "the teachings of ancient Egypt."

Regardless of knowing the reality behind its origin, alchemy is still present in today's world-consciousness. It is a power-ful philosophical and mystical tradition that covers a wide range of pursuits, topics, and practices.

Alchemy is so vast that if we were to write about it in its totality, 100,000 books wouldn't suffice. It also doesn't help that it's frequently presented with opaque language, further complicating an already dense topic. And the more abstract it gets, the more it hurts the practical process, leading to complex intellectual knowledge with no pragmatic utility.

Although alchemy has historically been used as a precursor to chemistry and modern science, the alchemy presented in this book is aligned with its original and intended intention: to decipher our spiritual nature beyond the physical dimension. Alchemists aim to transform and elevate themselves from the mundane dimension into the divine realm of reality.

Alchemy also seeks to heal, enlighten, and protect us from negative forces and influences. It empowers us and brings us into a state of heightened consciousness while also helping us be more effective, creative, and productive in our daily lives.

Ultimately, this mystical tradition provides transformation at the inmost level of our soul, giving each earnest practitioner greater light, power, and wisdom about themselves, the world, and the divine.

3

Inner vs Outer Alchemy

n the domain of dualism, there is a clear distinction between what each person would consider "himself" or "herself" and "not-self". Each student can easily identify what commonly constitutes both of these categories: your house, car, or this book fall under the "not-self" category, while your body, personality, or mind fall under the "self" category.

Whenever an alchemist attempts to create or change something exterior to themselves (the "not-self" category"), we can call it Outer, External, or Material Alchemy. An example of this would be changing some object, material, or substance into another (such as changing base metals into noble metals) or creating oils, tonics, medicines, and perfumes.

Contrastingly, whenever an alchemist is trying to change themselves or create something new within (the "self" category), we can call it Inner, Internal, or Spiritual Alchemy. There is a sharp contrast between the purpose of those who employ Outer Alchemy and those who search for wisdom and a higher degree of perfection and completion. Examples of Inner Alchemy would be a practitioner changing their inner chemistry, mental state, psyche, emotions, thoughts, habits, behaviors, vitality, body composition, creativity, energy, mood, and consciousness.

Any change a student desires can be accomplished, or at least initiated, through inner alchemical work. Whether a student intends to use Inner Alchemy to expand their artistic expression, increase work-related output, enhance mental abilities, empower individuality, or make a deep soulful spiritual transformation, the fundamentals and principles of alchemy will work. In fact, these principles apply to all dimensions of reality: physical, energetical, mental, and spiritual. They are the four main transformational phases when practicing Inner Alchemy.

Physical Alchemy

Strengthen and purify the body, and increase your well-being and longevity. Boost your health and immune system.

Energetical Alchemy

Clean and energize the energy pathways within the nervous system. Apply self-healing techniques to your body and its vital force, and sublimate sexual energy into mystical and spiritual endeavors. Work with the elements and fuse opposing energies to awaken the dormant primal power.

Mental and Psychological Alchemy

Vacate the mind, learn how to concentrate adequately, and achieve a thought-free state. Purify negative tendencies that habitually dwell within the psyche and delink thoughts and emotions from your conscious self. Awaken intuition and the inner eye, work with the elements, employ alchemical symbology, and use subtle forces. Gain more clarity regarding spiritual laws and how reality works. Treat psychological issues by probing into the subconscious, making the mind primed for the creation of the Philosopher's Stone.

Spiritual Alchemy

Connect with spiritual dimensions and achieve "alchemical gold" through the creation of the Philosopher's Stone. Employ profound alchemical procedures to embody transpersonal divinity. Spiritualize the body and materialize Spirit. Become your real self.

Through the alchemical process, students will not progress through these four transformational phases linearly because all phases interlace with each other, differing by grades of subtlety. As students advance through each stage, they will get a better understanding of their actual purpose on this planet and will have a clearer vision of how to follow through with it. More importantly, their soul, which is a manifestation of the divine, will finally be able to realize its deepest aspiration: become one with All That Is. This process is consistent with many mystical traditions that discuss transformation into higher states of consciousness and spiritual emancipation.

This work is fundamentally about Inner Alchemy, although it touches on every aspect of the art of alchemy. As the reader will discover, Inner Alchemy is much more than just something someone studies or reads: it requires putting knowledge into practice. And only those who are audacious will have the necessary willpower and discipline to perform the magic of alchemy to reach the far ends of this mysterious expedition.

4

Why has Alchemy been Distorted?

Alchemy is often the subject of ridicule: an old man working in a prehistoric fumy laboratory with numerous cylinders and glass spheres filled with bizarre liquids, analyzing obscure antique manuscripts in a hopeless crusade to transmute lead into gold. This is the view most people have once they hear the word Alchemy, and there's no point in denying it.

What was once the most mysterious, esoteric, and adventurous endeavor in the human realm is now seen as a pseudoscience hocus-pocus.

Although some alchemists did use laboratories for all

kinds of peculiar experiences, most of them were mystical adventurers of the inner realms and utilized a materialistic cover to escape prosecution and dodge accusations of what could be viewed as sacrilege.

The complex, allegorical, and oftentimes illogical vocabulary used in alchemical texts caused mass misinterpretation of what alchemy actually is. This is the main reason why alchemy has been distorted, twisted, misused, and mostly lost through time. The alchemical symbology, codes, images, and jargon were too complicated for the "uninitiated minds". Because of its esoteric nature, being shrouded by a play of words, riddles, and secrecy, and without adequate mystical depth, it is easy to become trapped in a maze of apparent nonsense. Those who have attempted to read ancient alchemical texts without a deep alchemical understanding know how difficult it is (and sometimes even futile) to get an approximate notion of what is being mentioned. There is virtually an impassable obscurity regarding substances' names, meanings, portions, purposes, etc. And that's to be expected because most alchemical texts were purposefully written to be as unintelligible as possible.

As a result of the low number of real alchemists at any time in any region, pseudepigrapha became the norm. Alchemy became full of falsely attributed texts, many of which used *Hermes Trismegistus* alias (a figure created by the syncretic admixture of the god Hermes and the god Toth; the alleged author of many ancient hermetic texts). If a student of the path didn't know better, they could've easily been misled by pseudo-alchemists. Yet behind the pretenders, there is a legitimate mystical discipline that can open the doors to the greatest enigmas of the self and the Universe.

Although fraudsters played a role in distorting alchemy, no one hurt it more than organized religion. Just like anyone with a known spiritual or scientific inclination would get persecuted by the Church, alchemists were also chased, oppressed, and even killed because of their heretical spiritual beliefs and disregard of Church dogma. That's why alchemists created the extremely convoluted materialistic "lead to gold" pretense.

Alchemy is a mystical practice that accentuates direct perception and experience of universal truths through practical methods. On the other hand, religion is man-made theology based on accepted beliefs about God or gods. Religion goes entirely against the principles of alchemy because it imposes its beliefs and doctrines onto a person without giving them appropriate tools to discover whether these beliefs are true or not. By studying alchemy, students read about what others have realized before them and, most importantly, learn the methodologies by which they can find out for themselves whether the universal truths and experiences alchemy discloses are fact or fiction.

Despite the numerous forms of alchemy, readers of this work should only focus on its most profound dimension: the alchemy of the soul (Inner Alchemy). Once it is found within, it can never be distorted or lost.

5

The Fundamental Laws

Every mystical tradition has its fundamental laws that carve its structure and teachings. Although there are apparent differences due to cultural and linguistic differences, these principles often point towards the same universal discoveries, regardless of the tradition. Notwithstanding the importance of these fundamental laws, they should not be blindly followed or seen as dogma. It's the responsibility of each practitioner to verify and confirm such precepts.

In Inner Alchemy, through the steadfast application of alchemical and mystical practices, students can explore and verify these universal principles for themselves. The failure to self-verify them will merely transform the beautiful process of Inner Alchemy into an esoteric doctrine.

Nonetheless, all students of Inner Alchemy must understand three fundamental principles before entering into the experimental phase. They're fairly intuitive, and there's a high likelihood that those who intend to initiate the practice of alchemy are already mindful of them.

Principle #1

The five senses show a limited perception of Reality

There is more than what you can see, taste, hear, smell, or touch. The five senses provide a limited experience of reality. A person whose view is only based on their limited sensory apparatus will believe that the material world is all there is. A completely materialistic outlook on the world typically makes people live from a completely consumerist perspective. As a result, most people try to gather as much money and material possessions as possible during their lifetime to increase their levels of satisfaction and pleasure, and prompted by the immature mind's desire to keep up a favorable social status among peers, succumb to its unenlightened will.

Although humanity has always perceived the Universe as having three dimensions and mostly being full of "inanimate matter", that is only a small side of Reality. The Universe is alive, conscious, and is a multi-dimensional reality. Each student must develop the needed mental abilities and discernment to perceive and experience these subtler dimensions of reality. Chances are that you've already had flashes of something beyond the five senses, and perhaps that's why you're reading this book.

Principle #2
There is an underlying source to everything that exists

Everything comes from a singular source, which can be named The One, God, The Primordial Substance, First Matter (although it's not "matter" in itself), Prima Materia, All That Is, Spirit, etc. This understanding pertains to all spiritual traditions, including Mysticism, Occultism, and Magick, which have been explored in the previous books of this series.

This source (God) is both the all and the nothing, the full and the empty, the light and the dark. But it is also beyond all of the dualism of these opposites. Nothing can confine God because both "confined" and "liberated" are just limited properties of a limited substance. God is not subject to anything. God is the rock, the one lifting it and the very act of successfully lifting it up. God is the rock, the one unable to lift it and the very act of failing to lift it up. God is truly limitless. God cannot be increased or decreased in any way, just like space. God will always and ever stay the same with no changes and no properties. Matter is just a small dimension of God that we perceive with our senses. It's the manifestation of the Beyond.

God is not a white man in the sky with a white beard and white vests sitting on a throne commanding the Universe. God is not a pagan figure, a religious deity, or any limiting and form-bound thing in itself. Whenever the word "God" is used in this book, it's not referring to any religious "god" but to the ungraspable formless source of everything that is.

Numerous alchemical books lack the appropriate commentary and elucidation regarding the Source. This is immensely significant because it is this understanding that will guide and direct students towards what they ultimately seek, and it will be expanded in later chapters of this book.

Principle #3

The source of unlimited power can be accessed from within

Our Quintessence, the divine spark that lives in each of us, is at the heart of alchemy. Each student has the capacity to penetrate the dense material layer of existence and discover the subtler levels of reality, both within and without.

The Universe, in its macrocosmic nature, inexhaustible in its vastness and mind-boggling in its mysteries, is incomprehensible to the human mind, so long as it confines itself to the physical senses. However, the microcosm, which is the universe inside of us that mirrors the external Universe, can be understood and realized through mystical practice, alchemical procedures, and spiritual contemplation.

The deeper our mind is into our subtle senses, the freer we are to assimilate Reality's mysteries and affect our lives in practical ways.

As above, so below, as within, so without,
as the universe, so the soul.

— Hermes Trismegistus

All of these three fundamental principles can be experientially unveiled by employing the art of alchemy. No student has to believe that there is more than what the five senses can perceive; they can discover this truth for themselves. There's absolutely no need to believe in the Source or formless "God" either; students merely have to unravel this underlying primordial Spirit in themselves. Inner Alchemy will allow them to explore the process of how God (formlessness) became matter (form), and how matter can become God once again. Alchemy provides a path to transmute our leaden self into pure limitless gold, and this cannot be confined to the domain of the mind but must be known by experience. This is what makes alchemy real.

SECTION 2

The Core

6

The First Matter

In the tradition of alchemy, *Prima Materia* (the "First Matter") is understood to be the primal source of everything. As we've already seen on the second universal principle of Inner Alchemy, this source, which is often called "God", is not an entity or an individual, although people all over the world attribute characteristics, features, emotions, traits, or even a personality to God, including students of alchemy.

Therefore, all students are free to use whatever name they see as most fit: The One, God, Spirit, All That Is, Universal Mind, Universal Consciousness, First Matter, Prima Materia, God-Consciousness, The Primordial Substance, Primordial

Self, the Self, Nothingness, Infinity, The Immutable, The Unfathomable, YHWH (יהוה), Father, Yahweh, Jehovah, Alpha and Omega, Allah, Hu, Bhagavan, Brahman, Shiva, Beingness, The Creator, etc. The name chosen will invariably be related to the culture or views of the student.

To understand the concept of the First Matter, we'll have to do the unthinkable: split God into two. But God cannot be split, students typically say. That is correct. But water cannot be split from its wetness either, yet we can divide them into "water" and "wetness" to explain them separately.

Similarly, because of God's inconceivable, unthinkable, and unknowable nature, we have to "split" Him to get to know Him to the best of our ability, in the context of alchemy.

God is both the Non-Matter and the First Matter. In its primordial non-form, before time, space, and Creation, God is nothing. God is nothing because it's not anything any student can perceive or experience. If a student were to perceive God through the limited human mind, it'd be no more than a futile attempt at trying to understand Infinity through finite instruments. On the other hand, in its First Matter form, God is the time, space, and Creation; He is everything. That's how God is nothing and everything at once. He's prior to Creation, and Creation itself latent with all of its potentiality.

Since God's primordial non-form cannot be known unless by inference after profound mystical practice, we have to focus on the First Matter. This First Matter is the Cosmic Force, God-Force, the Creative Power, the Vibration that ever-changes, the primordial Fire, the Universal Vital Force. If God unmanifested is Father, First Matter (God manifested) is Mother. She is the ecstatic divine presence that all students of mystical arts can experience through meditative training and the transcendental energy that transmutes the student's ego-self into Higher Self.

Seeing that no one can have water without wetness, by discovering, experiencing, and being one with the First Matter, what was seemingly impossible now becomes possible: the student becomes one with God's primordial formlessness.

The Egyptians represented the First Matter with this hieroglyph:

KH

It translates into *kh*, which is the first letter that makes up the word *khem*, the root of *Khemia*, which is not only the name the Greeks gave to ancient Egypt but also forms the root of the word Alchemy ("Al-Khemia").

This is the great secret of alchemy: Al-**KH**emia is the art of reconnecting with kh, the First Matter, God's Creation. The Great Work of Alchemy is connecting with the First Matter and using it to create the Philosopher's Stone. It is the art of being one with All That Is.

$$7$$

Alchemical Trinity

here are three fundamental components in alchemy that form the Alchemical Trinity: Sulfur, Mercury, and Salt. These components are frequently misunderstood, and if a student were to randomly open a book of alchemy and search for any of them, chances are that they'd be left wondering about their real significance and purpose.

It must be clear that these are not to be taken literally. They are not the chemical element or bright yellow crystal *sulfur*, the planet, Roman god, or chemical element *mercury*, or mineral *salt*.

Mercury and Sulfur are the Yin and Yang within each person: energy and consciousness, feminine and masculine, moon and sun, active and passive, motion and stillness. In each student's microcosm, Sulfur represents the principle of God's non-form (the still nothingness; the infinite still ocean of What Is; the Non-Matter; God-Consciousness), while Mercury symbolizes the principle of God's universal form (the motion of everythingness; the moving wave of What Is; the First Matter; God-Force). Salt represents the individuation, the ego-self.

Mercury (dynamic energy) acts as the medium between Sulfur (still consciousness) and Salt (ego). In Roman mythology, Mercury is the messenger between gods (Sulfur) and mortals (Salt). It represents the most powerful energy, the primordial Force, the ultimate Creative Power.

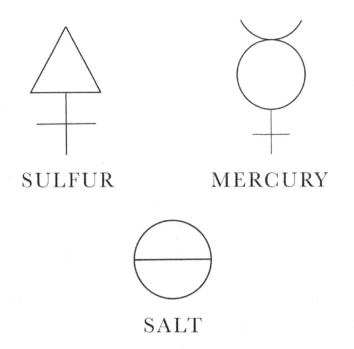

SULFUR   MERCURY

SALT

Salt is the principle of form. Through the union of Sulfur and Mercury, Salt materializes the unmanifested potential of God or Spirit. Salt (ego) is deemed corrupted or impure initially, inhibiting the soul from its freedom. Consequently, Salt must be purified (through alchemical practice) and reconstituted into pure Salt (divine Self; universal ego, Higher Self). It goes through an alchemical transmutation before crystalizing into its pure form. This alchemical work occurs predominately in the psychological realm, in the *Salt* that is the student's identity. Salt must be purified and dissolved before it can be "reassembled" as the student's true essence.

Behind the dense layer of Salt, at the center of the divine spark within each student, lies the microcosmic principles of Sulfur and Mercury. They are the two sides of the same coin and are depicted as a two-headed hermaphrodite.

Countless ancient alchemical texts from the likes of Paracelsus (one of the most well-known alchemists) identify these three components in alchemy and mention that merging Sulfur and Mercury create the third component: Salt. According to modern chemistry, they don't. But were Paracelsus and other alchemists wrong, or are they just being misunderstood?

Their main goal by merging Sulfur with Mercury was not to create table salt. The reason behind Paracelsus' desire to unite both principles within himself was to bring about purified Salt, which is another way of saying "enlightenment".

The microcosmic union of Sulfur and Mercury in each student creates this alchemical transmutation.

The alchemical vocabulary from ancient texts is fairly confusing, but that's why this work tries to decipher and break it down. A few hundreds of years ago, everything written here would be considered heresy and would lead you, the reader of this book, and myself, the author of this book, directly to the public guillotine, hanging, or we'd be burned at the stake. By codifying alchemy, creating complex jargon, special ciphers, and mixing Inner Alchemy with Outer Alchemy, no one but those in the known would understand what an alchemist was really writing about. Nobody would be able to discern that those alchemists were not talking about actual salt, mercury, and sulfur, but about subtle inner forces, states, and transformations. To outsiders, these writings were all nonsense or utterly unintelligible.

Nonetheless, using the analogy of water and wetness from the previous chapter on the Alchemical Trinity, students should understand the following:

The human psyche is mud (Salt). It contains water (Sulfur) and is evidently wet (Mercury), but it also contains soil, loam, clay, or silt (limitations and ignorance). Alchemists have to remove the soil, loam, clay, or silt from the mud to have pure water (pure Salt composed of only Sulfur-Mercury). Purifying and transmuting this mud (current self) until it becomes pure water (divine self) is the Great Work of Inner Alchemy.

The shackles of the ego (toad) prevent the soul (eagle) from flying freely towards the heavens of ecstasy.

- D. Stolcius von Stolcenberg, 1624,
Viridarium chymicum, Frankfurt am Main

8
_____

The Philosopher's Stone

The Philosopher's Stone is one of the biggest and most fascinating mysteries deeply buried in the collective consciousness of humanity. Seemingly out of reach, this miraculous Stone baffles the hearts and minds of those who seek it, enfolding them on a mythical journey towards an immeasurable treasure.

The teachings of the past show us that the Philosopher's Stone is not some fable or archaic bogus: it is real and capable of being created, contained in all things but seen by almost no one.

The Philosopher's Stone, mentioned in every alchemical work, was considered the key to creating gold through transmutation, but it also symbolized immortality and perfection. It may be looked upon as a token of physical immortality, but it also epitomizes the deathlessness of the soul. Its creation is often considered the crowning achievement of alchemy.

Few people consider the Philosopher's Stone real, but those who do are separated into two categories: students who believe it is an actual physical stone and students who interpret it as a spiritual transformation or enlightenment.

The first group sees the ancient texts literally, and they paint the Philosopher's Stone as a legendary alchemical dark red "material" capable of transmuting base metals into gold. They propose that it can also prolong life, heal all maladies, bring back any being from its ashes, or even produce otherworldly bodies.

The second group sees the Philosopher's Stone as an internal transmutation with physical, mental, and spiritual manifestations.

The inner alchemist sees all the esoteric explanations of alchemical compounds, solutions, salts, minerals, herbs, metals, and mechanisms as metaphorical expressions for inner states, mystical procedures, and metaphysical concepts. Despite reading about the achievement of bodily deathlessness, inner alchemists dig deep into their essence to uncover what was never born.

Outer Alchemy has some intriguing elements, but it's not conducive to profound inner transformation. All students of alchemy attracted towards alchemical laboratory work in hopes of creating a physical Philosopher's Stone should give it their honest attempt. However, they ought to know that they'll be working with all kinds of difficult-to-obtain toxic and sometimes deadly substances.

Although some alchemical literature has procedures that purportedly explain how to create the "stone", Inner Alchemy shows how to *be* it. The actual Philosopher's Stone is not a stone, but the materialization of a human being into their divine self; the transmutation into a pure manifestation of the First Matter. However, most students of alchemy will find the creation of the Philosopher's Stone an elusive attainment because it requires *years* of dedication, perseverance, and constant overtaking of plateaus where nothing seems to work.

Ultimately, only a few will get to the gold pot at the end of the rainbow. That's why it's one of the most remarkable achievements any human being can undertake.

9

The Three Marriages

It comes as no surprise that the central goal of classical alchemy is the physical creation of the Philosopher's Stone. Some alchemists used to spend most of their time in their laboratory working on compounds, or outdoors near sizeable furnaces heating substances for months and months, attentively distilling elements from different materials. More forward-thinking alchemists combined their outer practice with inner practice, creating a coexisting transmutation of themselves and the compound or substance being worked.

We won't go into the ins and outs of a literal laboratorium used for chemical transmutations. Despite the romanticism associated with alchemists, many of their procedures were not glamourous. Alchemists would frequently be using extremely toxic substances such as mercury, lead, or sulfur.

The intent of this work is not to teach you how to use mercury from the chemical supply store and wash it with rainwater multiple times, cover it with powdered sea salt, and let it digest in a hot furnace for countless months and months, trying to create the "Philosopher's Stone". It is not to learn how to distill urine or use feces or bodily fluids to create alchemical compounds either. You also don't need to utilize dried carcasses of rats or rabbits for self-transformational purposes. These were all methodologies many ancient alchemists employed.

Instead of living within a room that constantly smells like rotten eggs, alchemists of the inner world strive to go towards the euphoric perfume of the divine. They transcend rudimentary alchemical practices and adapt them towards contemporary students and alchemists.

Transmuting lead into gold is purely a figure of speech for the alchemical transformation that occurs on all levels of reality: physical, mental, and spiritual.

Ancient alchemical texts declare that there are three principal accomplishments or *Three Marriages* in the *Magnum Opus* (The Great Work of Alchemy) that affect each of these levels in different degrees of subtlety: Lunar Marriage, Solar Marriage, and Stellar Marriage.

1. Mind Union – Lunar Marriage

The personal mind unites with the First Matter/Universal Mind and temporarily transcends its body and limitations. This can be experienced by succeeding in the conjunction of Sulfur and Mercury.

2. Body Union – Solar Marriage

The energy and presence experienced in the Mind Union integrate into the alchemist's body. This is accomplished through the employment of the Inner Furnace method.

3. Spirit Union – Stellar Marriage

Owning to the union with and integration of the First Matter, what was seemingly impossible now becomes possible: the student becomes one with God's primordial formlessness. This ultimate transmutation manifests in the practitioner's self, transforming them into what's often called the *Philosopher's Child* or *the Self*. The individual soul is impregnated with the Universal Spirit.

The Lunar Marriage is likely to be the most consequential consummation for students of alchemy because it signals the first substantial step towards the Philosopher's Stone. Everything afterwards will come more naturally, although not without its ups and downs. Moreover, up until the Mind Union, many students depart from the alchemical path due to a lack of willpower, motivation, and evident results (mostly due to impatience). The winds will not always be advantageous to those who sail the caravel towards divinity, but it is the ones who persist that will find the promised land of alchemical gold.

Alchemical Symbology

Alchemy has some of the richest symbology out of all mystical traditions. It is so broad that there are books with over 700 pages packed with more than 1000 alchemical symbols and illustrations that cover only a part of alchemy. Some of these books do an outstanding job of explaining and interpreting ancient alchemical symbology, as it's typically fairly convoluted.

There are alchemical symbols for almost everything: substances, elements, metals, planets, dimensions, subtle forces, procedures, states, etc. However, profound iconographic exploration can quickly grow into an intellectual deviation. Because this volume favors practicality and contemporary understanding, students who wish to pursue Inner Alchemy just need to know and use a few symbols.

While some symbols are shared across distinct spiritual or religious traditions (despite being used or understood differently), others are unique to each student. Such symbols may spontaneously emerge in the student's mind during practice.

If that occurs, the student should follow their intuition; eventually, they'll get to comprehend the significance and purpose of that specific symbol, either by searching on metaphysical books, by asking their mystical or spiritual teacher, or through further inner exploration.

The five elements Earth, Water, Fire, Air, and Space are used in alchemy for a multitude of purposes. The last one can go by many different names, such as *Ether/Aether* (from Greek "the upper pure, bright air; firmament") or *Akasha* (the Sanskrit word for the concept of "sky" or "open space").

The 5th element is not God or the *First Matter*, as some alchemical works may lead the student to believe. It's an extremely subtle element, and it may be mistakenly seen as God or Spirit because it shares some characteristics with God, namely, being infinite, undestroyable, and omnipresent. Space is everywhere, and there's no end to it.

However, despite being very subtle, it is a manifested form, unlike God or Spirit, which is the underlying foundation or substance of all appearances, including those of a physical, energetic, mental, or causal nature, such as Space/Akasha.

Symbols and elements should not be taken literally but as a token of energy or elemental forces to be used in practice. Many have incorrectly interpreted them, predominantly with the ascent of contemporary chemistry.

In alchemy, elements are notably misunderstood. However, rather than reading a lengthy and theoretical breakdown about each of them and dabbling with hypothetical charades that restrict the student to the plane of belief and impracticality, the student will learn how to put them into use through pragmatic instructions in later chapters. In the mystical arts, too much theory distracts from the practice.

Alchemical symbols are only truly valuable if employed in practices to connect with subtle or archetypal energies. And that's precisely how Inner Alchemy incorporates them: as building blocks towards the creation of the Philosopher's Stone.

Alchemical Laboratorium

Unlike the widely believed alchemist laboratory, the *laboratorium* used for inner alchemic practice doesn't require a furnace or dried carcasses of rabbits or rats. It is a sacred space dedicated exclusively to the practice of alchemy; a space where anything except alchemical or mystical subjects, behaviors, or activities is viewed as "pollution".

It can be a whole infrastructure, such as a Temple, an entire division within a house, or a small space within a division. It can also be outside, as long as nobody can violate that space (i.e., it can't be a public park).

It is up to the student to choose according to their possibilities. Nonetheless, even a small space within a room, perhaps separated by a curtain, a screen (room divider), or something of a similar nature, is enough.

The laboratorium aims to facilitate the transmutation of the student's psyche. If a student of mystical arts arrives home from their job or from daily life in general, their common mental state of being will probably be very shallow, wandering around mundane matters.

The environment of a laboratorium conditions the student's mind to be focused, calm, and meditative. Just like someone might feel sleepy if they go to bed even if they weren't fatigued, the student will feel mystical ambition and inspiration and will be in the ideal state of mind to practice just by entering into this sacred space. It is the optimal place to practice. The laboratorium is such a powerful mystical mechanism (yet frequently overlooked) that it is transversal to all esoteric disciplines.

Here is what you should have in your laboratorium:

- A chair, a meditation cushion, or a mat if you favor practicing lying down.

You should practice while sitting in a comfortable position. It should not be too comfortable that you fall asleep, but it should not bring any degree of discomfort. The best options are sitting on a chair or on a meditation cushion with the legs crossed. As a last resort, you can practice lying down on your back, preferably not on your bed, to prevent the mind from falling into the usually conditioned reflex of falling asleep. Something like a yoga mat is preferred to lying down on the bed.

- Any object that helps you calm down your mind without making you over-externalize your attention is good.

E.g., A candle is a popular object because it is a universal symbol of calmness and introspection. Turn off any lights and let the natural flame of the candle illuminate the area. This sets up the ideal environment for alchemical practice.

Another item that you can use to make the room more suitable to practice is burning incense. This also helps to soothe the ambient. However, make sure the fragrance is not too strong that it turns into a distraction.

Fundamentally, any item that helps prepare the mind to enter into an environment conducive to inner practice is good. Anything that distracts the mind must be disposed.

The same is valid for sound. Some students favor practicing with some meditative music, nature sounds, binaural beats, or even with the sound of a water fountain.

Note: if you can't pick a noise-free environment due to outside noise, you can treat the outside noise as thoughts and therefore ignore them, use sounds as mentioned above, or you can use silicone earplugs.

All of the items used within the laboratorium must be used exclusively there. They cannot have any other purpose, or they will lose their intention and energy.

As the journey progresses, new objects or substances will naturally be added to your laboratorium, working synergistically with your current practice. In addition, students with a more devotional disposition can also use an object that signifies their devotion towards God or towards the higher goal they're trying to achieve. Before each practice, contemplate this object and its meaning for a few minutes to increase your devotion and, therefore, your motivation and inspiration to practice. This devotion-object must be treated just like all objects within the laboratorium: with respect and reverence, making them sacred.

Some alchemical books use the term *oratorium* (oratory; the place of prayer) instead to differentiate from *laboratorium* (laboratory; the place of labor). The oratorium was used to pray or meditate and the laboratorium to perform alchemical transmutations. But because the substance of transformation is the body, mind, and self, our place of prayer is the same as the place of labor: ourselves.

10

Black, White, and Red

Alchemy is an intricate metaphysical system with complex symbology, and it has left an enduring legacy in human history and culture. But perhaps more importantly, alchemy speaks to us on an elemental level. All a student needs is some basic understanding of alchemy and how to practice it to get started.

However, the difficulty with learning alchemy is that alchemists deliberately muddled their inner practices, techniques, methodologies, and processes to misguide the uninitiated. They created a complicated system while camouflaging the true subject matter rather than going straight to the point and explaining the legitimate methods. Multiple works attempt to explain these systems through different angles, but they are often significantly dense and discouraging to the neophyte. With this in mind, this volume will attempt to elucidate and clarify each step along the alchemical path while using a contemporary and well-defined approach that stays loyal to the ancient methodologies and practices of Inner Alchemy.

There are three main allegorical phases in the path of alchemy: Blackness ("Nigredo"), Whiteness ("Albedo"), and Redness ("Rubedo"). Black is the first phase of the path, White the second, and Red the final one. Alchemists used these three colors because they were also the sequential pigments occurring when working with metals.

Although some ancient alchemical literature elaborates on those phases through processes such as calcination, dissolution, sublimation, separation, fermentation, putrefaction, etc., there's insufficient cohesion and uniformity concerning their order, description, or use. Furthermore, they've largely been addressed as mechanisms of creating substances, medicines, etc. Seeing that Inner Alchemy is concerned with transforming the alchemist's self, we will penetrate beyond these processes' superficial connotations and use them as inner mechanisms of transformation. Sometimes, the student will go through them without even noticing. This is preferable to blurring the students' minds with more concepts, distractions, and possibly giving an opaque and extremely dense view of alchemy. Most students quit and don't even attempt to put alchemy into practice when faced with so much information and esoteric lexicon.

Black Phase

The Black Phase is the initial and most strenuous stage in the path of Inner Alchemy. In this phase, students will purify their body, emotions, and mind; they'll have to purge all of the "darkness" within themselves, letting go of everything that holds them back from deeper alchemical and mystical work. This purifying work can take many years to accomplish, and it's where most students get stuck.

Before undertaking a mystical journey, most people are in a state of distress, even if they're not truly mindful of it. They spend their whole lives just getting by and appear to look fine from the outside. However, that is merely a facade, and inwardly, they feel incomplete and wrecked. They try to accomplish what society tells them they need: an appropriate job, a loving partner, etc. But even when they seem to be triumphing, the smoke of joy quickly fades away, and they're left with a vacuum inside. However, when some rare individuals notice that the pleasures found in life cannot give them what they are searching for, they look for other ways.

Every student of alchemy knows that there's a deeper dimension to life, one that people do not usually talk about because most of them are unaware of it. This dimension has a different type of profundity, and it is available to all students of mystical arts.

But in all spiritual paths, students begin from dark ignorance. In this stage, they have many flaws, their psyche has yet to be purified, and they lack the mental ability and fortitude to probe deep into their inner world.

Most of the gross impurities and pollution in the student's body, energy-bound emotions, and mind ought to be removed in the Black Phase. Otherwise, the more advanced stages will be completely inaccessible as the student will lack the required mystical development and experience.

Once these gross contaminants have been burned and dissolved, the student must discover and face the darker side of their personality, which is often called "the shadow." This side of you lurks below the conscious mind in the murky dark waters of the psyche and surfaces now and then, silently shaping many of your decisions and behaviors, even if it conflicts with your values and way of acting. A great deal of suppressed or buried content must be brought to light and overcome.

The Black Phase culminates in burning and dissolving this psychological darkness to begin exposing the underlying essence of light. Because there's an initial probing into the subconscious to unveil and purify the psychological processes within the practitioner's psyche, the attentive student must pay special attention to prevent these traumas and negative energies from taking control of the mind and directing it to a state of meaninglessness or purposelessness. Do not inhale the toxic haze of the blackening phase but purify it and let it pass to reach the next stage.

White Phase

After the initial purification of gross substances in the Black Phase, students must now surrender their ego to light. The inner darkness was destroyed, and now it's time to transmute the psyche and integrate it.

Students will empower their purified being by raising their energy and mind to a higher intensity and presence. They will learn how to discriminate their identity and its underlying nature while also merging the opposite poles of masculine and feminine energy.

This is a lengthy intermediate phase. However, unlike the Black Phase, which can be particularly daunting, dry, or relentless, the White Phase is more rapturous and exhilarating, with mystical states and otherworldly discoveries that get assimilated into the body, energy, and mind.

With the awakening of the Secret Fire, spiritual light will emerge within the alchemist's body, and the "metal to gold" transformation will become more noticeable, as the spiritual light suffuses and envelops them in a yellow-golden color, which indicates the transition from the white to the red phase.

Red Phase

In this conclusive phase, alchemists will sublimate and refine the material and the spiritual within themselves, coagulating into a new self. Body, energy, mind, and spirit will unite to transmute the base metal-self into pure gold-self. Some methods applied in the Red Phase will ensure that no impurities or submerged shadow from the previous identity laying around in potentiality within unconscious parts of the psyche infiltrate into the manifestation of the new self on the coagulation process.

As you approach the final steps of creating the Philosopher's Stone, a higher intelligence will begin influencing you with thoughts and perceptions that will assist you in the quest for alchemical enlightenment. This intuition comes from your actual self and becomes unmistakably audible as you reach new peaks of spiritual growth. This also leads to alchemical fermentation, which is when a profound desire for alchemical and mystical success is cultivated and nurtured within the alchemist with such strength that it causes a tangible change in their whole being. A living inspiration that surfaces from the depths of the nonphysical dimension as a result of assiduous practice and devotion to the goal is the best form of fermentation.

This phase climaxes in the creation of the Philosopher's Stone: alchemists unleash the alchemical dragon and become the living proof of the First Matter.

SECTION 3

The Training

11

Initial Alchemical Practice

It is well known that the alchemist's goal is to create the Philosopher's Stone. However, the purpose of Inner Alchemy goes behind that: it's not so much to create the Philosopher's Stone but to become the living Philosopher's Stone.

To become the living Philosopher's Stone, students have to perform a set of mystical and alchemical procedures that aim at transforming the four main dimensions of human existence: physical, energetical, mental, and spiritual.

The more consistent a student is with their daily practice, the more second nature and effortless that habit becomes. After a while, it even becomes a necessity; the daily allocation of time to practice alchemy becomes as essential as eating or sleeping.

The ensuing alchemical practices will guide the student towards the *Magnum Opus* and mystical emancipation. Each phase has its specific alchemical preparation and methodology.

Keep in mind that there are variations of these methods as they present themselves slightly different according to the tradition of each teacher and their mystical path. Alchemy is a wide-ranging and all-encompassing tradition, so there will always be interdisciplinary procedures with parallel mechanisms.

The key to Inner Alchemy lies in practice.

Physical Alchemy

The physical body is the student's vessel in this world. Therefore, alchemical work must begin with the body: you have to transform it together with your energy and mind, as they work in harmony. None must be left behind.

The more pristine and spiritually refined a physical body is, the more freely energy circulates in it and the less mental fog the student experiences, subsequently having more clarity and energy. With more clarity and energy, a deeper form of alchemy can be practiced, and the Philosopher's Stone created. Although most of these changes occur within, they're eventually manifested externally, both in the body and life of the student.

Understanding the physical body and how it affects the mind and energy is an ability that comes as a student continuously deepens their inner alchemical practice. Although the main objective is to connect with the First Matter, that can only be attained if the student first purifies and transforms their body, energy, and mind. For all of this to materialize, the student must begin by purifying their body through physical alchemy. Physical alchemy is transforming the physical body.

There are three essential components that the student must focus on to transform the physical body: food, exercise, and sleep.

a) Food

Students of alchemy should eat a healthy and balanced diet with an adequate water intake.

Plant-based food is not a requirement, but the fewer meats a student eats, the better. Meat digestion is energetically demanding, so students should take that into deliberation. Every student should pay attention and see how their food choices affect their body and mind.

Regarding body weight, the recommendation is to change the caloric intake until the student is satisfied with their weight. However, students are not advised to follow unbalanced lifestyles. Nobody would disagree that having a healthy body is better for our well-being, mind, and energy, though obsessions over body fitness are not only required but should be avoided. Moderation is the dictum.

b) Proper exercise

Physical exercise is one of the most meaningful things anyone can do for their well-being. Students ought to practice some exercise; even if the only exercise a student does is walking for 30 minutes per day, that would be good. Low-intensity cardiovascular exercises are beneficial to the heart, while resistance training or bodyweight exercises (e.g., squats, push-ups) are also exceptional for the body and bone density. Lastly, the weekly practice of yoga asanas or flexibility exercises can help keep the body flexible and elastic.

c) Adequate sleep hygiene

Sleep is the third pillar of physical alchemy. Good sleep helps the body recover and rejuvenate, and it also helps rest the conscious mind. If a student doesn't get adequate sleep, they will doze off during internal practices. Furthermore, there are a host of problems associated with sleep deprivation or bad sleep hygiene. There is a prevalent hustle culture in some circles where sleep gets discarded for the sake of having more time to work, which can be extremely destructive to a person's physical and mental health. Sleep is essential, and students of alchemy must remember this.

With adequate food, exercise, and sleep hygiene, the student's body will not only be a powerhouse of health but will be primed for alchemical practice.

Despite these guidelines, self-enforcing strict rules regarding diet change or exercise can be counterproductive. It is in your best interest to observe a reasonable lifestyle according to your goals and inclinations. Keeping balance is every student's duty.

Preventive care is the most important approach that we can have towards our bodies. Despite tremendous advancements in today's medicine, there's a never-ending profit-seeking to make the next drug and sell it. Although it is out of the scope of this book, there are numerous alchemical medicines made from plants that may be beneficial. Interested students are advised to look into herbal medicine.

After taking care of food, exercise, and sleep, your body will begin to change. These three steps can be reoriented towards the right direction in a matter of days or weeks. But you don't have to wait for "perfection" to go further into alchemy; once you are on the right direction in regard to the transmutation of the physical body (i.e., you're making the necessary changes to harmonize your body with these three steps), you can begin the next stage of alchemical practice, which aims to "burn" physical tension points and then dissolve them away.

Procedure:

1. Sit down with a good posture or lie down, take a deep breath, and relax.

2. While inhaling, tense your feet, feel a slight burn sensation, and then while exhaling, relax them while feeling like cool water energy dissolves the tension. Next, take another breath in and tense your calves, feel a slight burn sensation there, and then relax them while breathing out and feeling the tension being dissolved by cool water energy. Keep doing this method of inhaling and tensing with a slight burning sensation, and exhaling and releasing these muscles with cool water energy, and apply it to the thighs, hips, glutes, stomach, chest, upper back, hands, arms, neck, jaw,

face, and head. Pay particular attention to the relaxing motion and feeling of cool water energy when you let your muscles completely relax after tensing them.

3. Continue doing this for 2-3 rounds to get your muscles fully relaxed. If possible, wear loose and comfortable clothing. Tight clothes may restrict blood circulation and the flow of energy.

The ability to relax the body is a skill just like any other, and it can be learned progressively. In the beginning, it will take a lot of time to relax deeply, and it can lead to sleep, boredom, dreaming, etc., diminishing your enthusiasm. But if you approach it with the correct mindset, you will achieve a good degree of deep physical relaxation in a few weeks.

The objective of this exercise will be accomplished if the student has managed to relax each body part deeply. Given sufficient practice, you will be able to achieve this state quickly at the beginning of each practice session. Profound physical relaxation allows you to enter into mystical states more easily and perform Inner Alchemy within your psyche. In this state, the student's consciousness operates at a much higher level, and because of this, all of their mystical or alchemical practices will be much more powerful and efficient.

Energetic Alchemy

Energy is a key component in alchemy, and there are multiple forms of it: physical energy, emotional energy, mental energy, elemental energy, universal energy, vital energy, and so on. This phase uses the vital energy or force inherent to each human being.

The vital force is the subtle form of breath; it is the "breath of life", the energy that runs through your nervous system (or energy body). Many ancient alchemists held the vital force as a substance that they could extract or isolate from living beings (e.g., animals, plants), preserve, and use for various purposes. However, there is a much better way of accomplishing this, particularly when the intention is spiritual progress. As living creatures, we all possess the vital force within us, and we just need to know how to use it.

Before plunging deeper into alchemy, students must first identify the vital force within themselves and then learn how to apply it to clean the energy pathways in their nervous system. This fundamental process is highly purifying and transformative. It may not seem like much, but real depth won't be achieved without the awareness of the vital force. Mastery over it opens up millions of doors in alchemy and other mystical disciplines.

In ancient times, many priests used to firmly believe in the adage "Ora Et Labora". This means "to pray and work". Since we are the main subject of the art of alchemy, the inner laboratory where we perform most of our alchemical work will be the temple of our prayer.

Alchemists use fire as their primary tool of transformation, and it should come as no surprise that many alchemists and hermeticists were called Fire Philosophers. The fire used by them was three-fold: actual visible fire, invisible fire, and the Secret Fire (also called the "mother" Kundalini-Shakti in ancient Sanatana Dharma).

Actual visible fire is important because it's utilized to prepare and create alchemical compounds and medicines. However, our interest lies more in the invisible fire and the Secret Fire. The first is our personal or individual vital force or *prana*, while the latter is the universal or transpersonal vital force (our microcosmic principle of Mercury). Beginning the process of awakening the student's perception of the invisible fire, and learning how to control it, is the purpose of this practice.

In most students, this fire has been mostly asleep. To become aware of it, the student must use their imagination as a "portal" to the actual sensing of the vital energy.

Procedure:

1. Sit down in a comfortable position, close your eyes, and relax your body by inhaling through the nose and exhaling through the mouth.

2. Do this for around five minutes.

3. Once you are relaxed enough, visualize radiant white energy rising from the bottom of the spinal cord, going upwards around the back until the top of the head while inhaling, and then going down through the front of the body while exhaling until it reaches the coccyx.

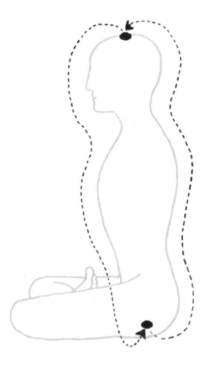

This energy will begin to surround your whole body until you get into a deep and relaxed, energetic state. Your body may also start to feel very light.

Do this for 10 to 20 minutes.

Given sufficient practice, you will begin to sense the vital force within your body and aura (an extension of the energy body). You may start shivering at the energy flowing through the spinal cord or feel a sensation of burning, tingling, or numbness all over the body, or any type of energetic effect. This agitation or stirring up of the vital force stimulates the trapped or inactive energy to animate and circulate.

This is how a student begins to become aware of the vital force within themselves. This awareness used to be dark, but it is now brought to light.

Notice that your vital energy is just a small part of the grand and vast universal energy, just like the space inside a jar is but a small part of the universal space that fills the whole universe.

Once you can distinctly sense the invisible fire, your procedure will have a slight modification: instead of visualizing and feeling the energy going upwards around the back until the top of the head while inhaling, and then going down through the front of the body while exhaling, you will feel it go both upward and down through the spinal cord.

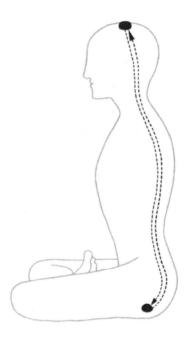

With this modification, you will clean your energy pathways within the body. It may appear simple, and it is, but it's critical work. Variations of this technique are at the core of various yogic or mystical practices.

The more the energy consciously flows through your spinal cord, the more you will purify your energy body by "burning" through energetic impurities and preparing it for the awakening of the powerful Secret Fire at the base of the spinal cord.

Mental Alchemy

Just like the physical alchemy's purpose is to purify and transform the body and energetic alchemy to purify and transform energy, the purpose of mental alchemy is to purify and transform the mind. Through this initial stage of mental alchemy, the student will employ alchemical practices to perfect their mind and personality, and mature their psyche. This initial mental stage is indispensable and should be practiced with exceptional diligence. A disorganized and untrained mind cannot handle the more powerful mental alchemical procedures; the mind mustn't be a lawless space but the nucleus from where the neophyte starts creating the Philosopher's Stone.

The body, energy, and mind must be trained concurrently, gradually refining without hastening any part over the other. The mental and psychological work is probably the hardest to succeed, but it's essential. You need to quieten your mental space and awaken the inner eye and intuition before you can purify the unconscious roots that bind you to a self-fulfilling cycle of suffering and dispel negative tendencies that habitually dwell within your psyche.

At first, the mind will likely be in a state of disorder and tumult. However, if you've already been practicing the previous two forms of Inner Alchemy for some time, or if you practice mental alchemy right after practicing physical alchemy and energetic alchemy (combining all three in a single session), your mind will be in a higher state of equilibrium than usual.

Procedure:

1. Light up a candle, sit down comfortably and relax the whole body.

2. Observe the candle for a few minutes, slowing down your breathing.

3. Close your eyes and observe your mind for five minutes. Try to get a picture of how your mind works. Is it chaotic, peaceful, or something in-between?

Initially, you will discover that thoughts come from everywhere; they are about everyday occurrences, work-related issues, plans for tomorrow, etc. Silently observe these thoughts without being absorbed by them. Don't let yourself fall asleep. If you are too fatigued, this means that you are not performing physical alchemy correctly because you're supposed to practice good sleep hygiene.

If instead of feeling lethargic, you feel agitated, then it is an issue of relaxation. You must go back to physical alchemy and master the relaxation process. Burn all of the tension, dissolve it with cool water energy, and then your consciousness will sink into a deep mental state, and restlessness will not be an issue.

Can you dictate that you shall have no thoughts for a few minutes? How can a student expect to succeed at a high level of inner alchemical practice if they have no control over their mind?

You ought to keep observing thoughts for five minutes, increasing the time as you feel comfortable until you reach ten to twenty minutes. Those who so desire may go up to thirty minutes.

Even though many thoughts will appear throughout the session, they will begin to dissolve when you "look" at them, giving birth to a mental vacuum. From one session to the next, you will notice that the mental chatter becomes progressively less turbulent until only a couple of thoughts emerge in your mind.

This practice must be given intense attention because a composed mind is fundamental for deeper alchemical work. Unfortunately, achieving a truly serene mind is considerably challenging, and that's why countless aspirants eventually relinquish the process at this stage. But students shouldn't overlook this step, and on no account should they proceed further into alchemical practice until this one is sufficiently mastered.

Through this method, you will condition your mind to burn and dissolve most or all of your mundane thoughts and superficial mental impulses that may disturb you from achieving deeper states during practice. A meditative and empty mental space will become the new standard every time you practice.

When you can consistently experience a complete withdrawal from your typical mental state with only a few or no thoughts roaming around the mind for around five minutes, you can graduate into the next step. This profoundly relaxed yet vigilant state is indispensable because the next step requires that you concentrate on a single image or thought without wandering.

You can use any thought, image, letter, symbol, etc., to practice. Nonetheless, it is recommended that you pick a symbol or image connected to alchemy, such as the symbol of the Fire element (a triangle).

Close your eyes and visualize the chosen symbol. Firmly refuse everything unrelated to the selected object of concentration, and hold it vigorously to the best of your ability.

You will only manage to do so for a few seconds at the start. However, you will become better at holding a single thought or image through assiduous practice. The skill to hold a specific image or thought in your mind and then using it to imprint energy into an alchemical procedure is another essential component of the mental alchemical process. Keep on practicing with great perseverance.

Alchemical Bonfire

One of the elemental principles of alchemy is that anything superficial or impure has to be dissolved to reveal its underlying essence. "Boiling the King Alive" is a typical alchemical metaphor and symbol, which means "Dissolving the Ego". Instead of ruling us, the ego-king is sacrificed to the greater good of our self.

The calcination and dissolution of the impurities within the mind is the last step of this phase. And at the core of all these impurities lies the ego.

Nonetheless, sacrificing the king is an onerous and complicated task because like the term "sacrificing" indicates, it seems like you will lose the game. Sacrificing the king can be exceptionally tricky, so all students have to approach it delicately. It is a multistage procedure.

In this subprocess, you will use the Fire element to burn your inner blackness into ashes. We all have something that obstructs the light from within, and it must vanish. This burning can be the natural effect of the previous practice if the student has chosen the symbol of Fire, or the student can be the one to initiate it.

To do so, visualize the elemental symbol of Fire (Δ) transforming into a flame that envelopes your body with heat and fire as if it were burning off all of your impurities and darkness, which are released from your mind as black smoke.

Do this until you begin to feel intense heat all over your body.

Once the heat is tangible, centralize the fire in your head and intensify it. This fire amplifies the mental process of purification, roasting the mind of its contaminants. See the blackness coming out as black smoke while you simultaneously feel lighter and lighter.

Do this procedure for as long as you can, but never for less than 20 minutes, always imagining and feeling the impurities and blackness coming out through the black smoke.

Every person has subconscious smog that clashes with their current consciously chosen direction. Dissolving these fabricated structures that operate as ego-surviving mechanisms requires that the student emerges their conscious mind into the dark waters of the unconscious.

After purifying with fire, the ego-king's control is surrendered, bringing buried material and suppressed energy and emotions into the forefront of your mind. These energies and thoughts must be de-linked entirely from your emotional investment and then dissolved and transmuted from dark, repressed material into bright, positive energy. The surfaced material may take the form of visions, mental images, unusual thoughts, bizarre feelings, or murky energies. Instead of ignoring it, you should intentionally analyze it without any emotional involvement, letting it "dry out".

Continue this daily practice for at least three months or until you experience such mental transmutations.

In laboratory-based alchemy, if the practitioner uses too much liquid in this stage, the matter used tends to decay or rot. In the internal laboratory of mental alchemy, uncontrollable emotions and repressed feelings are the liquid that will try to putrefy your mind. Facing your own psychological shadow may give rise to feelings of guilt, disgrace, remorse, or shame, but you'll have to be as serene as possible and, with bravery and resilience, disassociate yourself from the severe gripping effect of those powerful emotions deeply rooted within the psyche. The inner heating evaporates these harmful liquids and gives the student an opportunity to transcend the deadly smoke of the buried material.

All of these events or feelings may surface unexpectedly during or after the practices. Getting rid of the gross impurities that chained the psyche will finally liberate the spark of light trapped within. Free at last.

12

Deep Alchemical Practice

In the prior phase, the student got rid of numerous harmful thinking habits, disruptive beliefs, projections, and rejected material. The old personality that the student used to know is now broken, and the previously veiled light now gleams through the cracks.

The first phase led students to deal with their own "shadow", while this one leads them to deal with their own "light". In this phase, the student has to unify and transmute the "essences" that survived the previous purification and transformations to transcend the core of their identity and bring the inner light to the front. This moment is gratifying because it signals a shift from the Black Phase into the

White Phase; it's the beginning of the second phase of Inner Alchemy. The vital force roams more freely within the nervous system, and the mind doesn't inhabit the realm of uncontrollable and obstructive thoughts anymore. It is the dawn of a new mindset and outlook, free of its gross impurities.

Unlike other forms of personality-perfecting alchemy, deep alchemical practice deals with transpersonal transformation and subtle universal forces that can be harnessed to transmute our whole being.

Light your flame and go deeper.

Alchemy of the Psyche

In the previous energetic and mental stages, the student purified the most unsuitable gross material. Now, they have to filtrate the remaining polluted components and retrieve the essential constituents.

To carry out the transmutation of the identity, the student must isolate, purge, and refine what was left of their identity to recover its essential element: the First Matter. Furthermore, the student will also have to dissect and discern the underlying duality of the contents of the psyche by using the energy of the Air element. This discrimination of the inner world will allow the student to cultivate opposing forces within their energy body and later awaken the sacred Fire energy, generating unthinkable amounts of power.

Isolating the core of the ego and its unwanted structure will help facilitate the separation of what "self" is from what "self" isn't; we become cognizant of what we are and what we aren't. By deeply penetrating the foundation of the mind, we'll uncover the essential subject that undergoes this alchemical quest. This revelation enables us to connect with the First Matter within ourselves (the microcosmic principle of Mercury) and transmute the false and fragmented identity into a whole and integrated sense of self.

Air is essential for this procedure because it links the student's personal subconsciousness and the universal unconscious layer of Creation. This layer is not personal like an individual mind, but collective, being in some form or another present in all individual life forms. It has structures and processes which are shared and present in every one of us.

Preparation:

Although we primarily focus on Inner Alchemy, there are some practices where ancient outer alchemical methods and compounds can be valuable to our journey.

In this alchemical practice, you will learn how to create a liquid compound and use the power of the Air element to charge it. This procedure will assist you in separating your false self from the real you.

Every utensil, recipient, or object used here must be thoroughly sanitized and purified. To sanitize them, you can use any method of choice (e.g., using bleach, hydrogen peroxide, a disinfecting solution, or boiling the utensils in water for 10 minutes). To purify or consecrate them, perform a simple process of focusing on each item separately and imprint them with the same "alchemical energy" that you typically feel in your alchemical laboratorium.

This process also requires a source of heat, like an open flame. It could also be something like a stove if there is no alternative. Most students won't be able to have a fire in their laboratorium, so they will have to carry out the procedures using actual fire elsewhere. If possible, it's advisable to do it outdoors (always with extreme care not to start a fire).

However, if it has to be done in another room (e.g., in the kitchen where there is a stove), try to purify that division similar to what you did with the utensils.

The best alchemical compounds are prepared from various plants and materials with active and robust properties. But not all liquids or objects are suitable to receive and be charged with an intention or energy. Gold is a powerful energy conductor, so the student is advised to get a gold tincture (or dilute 1 gram of gold chloride in 20ml or 0.7 ounces of distilled water) and pour 5 to 15 drops into 100ml or 3.5 ounces of water in a small container. Let it saturate the water for about 30 minutes.

As a substitute, you can produce this tincture yourself as ancient alchemists did:

1. Get a piece of gold and a large container of distilled water (at least 15 times the weight of the gold).

2. Heat the gold in an open flame until it is red, and then put it into the distilled water. Don't let anything but the gold touch the water (but be careful of getting splashed by the water). Let it cool down. Take the piece of gold out of the large container of distilled water with any utensil, but make sure it has been adequately cleaned and disinfected in advance.

3. Repeat this process eight times. Minuscule gold particles are released each time you do it, and the water will
become saturated with gold particles.

Once this process is finished, you can pour 5 to 15 drops
of this substance into 3.5 ounces or 100ml of distilled water.

To create the alchemical fluid, you first need to get a
handful of rose leaves or blossoms, hazel leaves, and cham-
omile flowers (in equal parts). These can easily be found in
the wild, in herbal stores, or ordered online.

Mash them, and then cover them with water on a pot
with a lid. Once they are mostly submerged, boil them for
15 to 20 minutes.

While the herbs are boiling, focus on the contents inside
the pot and charge them with the Air element [△].

Inhale deeply with your eyes closed, and when exhaling,
open your eyes and let the pranic-air energy leave through
your hands into the pot, charging with the element of Air.
Use the power of your imagination.

Do this for the entire 15 to 20 minutes.

Afterwards, when the water has cooled down and the herbs are dissolved, filter about half of the water out and keep the decoction within the pot.

To be better preserved, add around 2oz or 60ml of pure alcohol to the herbs/liquid. Next, add 10 to 15 drops of the gold tincture mixture that you've created earlier (some alchemists use drops of their own blood here instead of gold). Mix it well and pour it into a proper recipient that can be hermetically sealed.

This recipient should be kept in a cool, dry place out of direct sunlight, and it won't lose its potency for a long time.

Most alchemical liquid compounds created like this can be used for the intended effect. Even if it looks like a foolish process, their alchemical impact will be tangible, particularly when combined with inner alchemical practices. Plant extracts can be quite potent if used correctly; it is not surprising that substances like morphine, caffeine, or aspirin, among countless others, come from plants.

Procedure:

1. Grab a small piece of paper and write something that describes or defines who you are; something that you identify with, or your story or personality. You can use only keywords if you desire. Furthermore, if you are more of a "visual person", you can also draw a picture, a symbol, or something representing your personality and story. Invest emotional energy into it. Take your time.

2. Draw the Salt symbol on the blank side of the paper. It represents your ego, identity, or individuality. It's a circle separated in the middle. The circle represents wholeness, God, or indivisibleness, but it's currently divided to create dualism or symbolize the separation between self and the

not-self. If you want to draw it using a pair of compasses and a ruler, remember to purify them beforehand.

3. Use your hands and crush the paper together, compacting it until it's a small, crumpled paper ball.

4. Put the paper ball into a small recipient and add a few drops of the alchemical fluid that you've created in the preparation into the paper.

5. Burn the paper (alone, preferably outside). You can do it in various ways, such as by grabbing the paper with a purified fireplace tong and setting it on fire with a lighter purchased exclusively for this purpose. You can burn it in a fireplace if you do it indoors.

6. Concentrate on the burning paper with the intention of letting your story and ego-personality fade away with the smoke; let them dissipate; let your false self go; let the universal Air element absorb it.

7. Once the paper is fully burnt, grab the ashes, and dispose of them into a body of water, preferably the ocean or a river.

In each student, the ego is merely a mental construct, like ripples in a vast body of water. It possesses a story and a personality that hide the underlying substance of the real Self. The essence of the Alchemy of the Psyche is not achieved only through this alchemical procedure, but it provides a vital help both in terms of energy and subconscious transformation.

Once this process is concluded, sit in your favored meditative posture, in your habitual place of practice, and attempt to identify in your mind what constitutes your self. Are you that "thing" that you are identifying? How can you be limited to it? How can a mental construct confine your whole sense of self?

Mud is composed of clay, loam, or silt mixed with water. If you believe you are mud, you cannot discover your divine nature as pure, dazzling clear water. Alchemy helps you purify the mud until only your original state of pure water remains. Fortitude, determination, and diligence are indispensable conditions to this process.

Repeat the whole process twice a week for an entire year for the best results.

This process of self-investigation will work as a final purgation of impurities, removing any contamination or potential ego-residues in the psyche. You will break the shackles that blocked you from feeling and being free. It's an indispensable preamble to the rebirth of the student in a more faultless and pure state of being.

The Conjunction of Sulfur and Mercury

The Roman god Mercury is often depicted holding a staff with two snakes entwined in opposite directions around it. This staff, called the caduceus, is also the primary symbol of Hermes, the Greek herald of gods.

In alchemy, the caduceus represents the awakening and rising of the universal vital force through alchemical transmutations. Alchemists call this vital force the "Secret Fire" or "Spirit's Pure Energy" to differentiate it from our own "personal" vital force. It's the *Kundalini* from Hinduism or the *Holy Spirit* from Christianity.

The two opposite serpents are the opposing energies that must be elevated and merged to allow the student to experience union with the First Matter. When they rise and merge, the Secret Fire ascends through the middle of the Staff. The two wings illustrate the ascension of consciousness to divinity.

Mercury is the dynamic principle of the divine, as explained in chapter 8, and what ultimately guides the student back towards the unblemished divine state.

You will use your purified vital force to awaken the Secret Fire and ascend through the Staff towards the wings of freedom. The energy within your body and mind contains all the ingredients required to fuel the necessary transmutations and attain this goal.

However, in this particular practice, the method doesn't lie in elevating the opposing energies and then merging them, but in first merging them and only then elevating them. Merging the opposite energies and elevating them through the "middle of the Staff" (i.e., the spinal cord) will stir up the Secret Fire and awaken it. When the Secret Fire rises through the Staff, the wings of freedom will take you to the heavens.

Alchemy is only that which makes the impure pure by means of Fire.

— Paracelsus

There are three alchemical methods to achieve this: The Yoke Method, The Fire Method, The Union Method.

The Yoke Method:

This method will be the best method for the majority of students. It's a technique that progressively arouses the Secret Fire until it awakens while minimizing energetic overload. It requires diligence and devotion to the practice.

Technique #1

This practice requires the knowledge of the location of the seven main energy centers (called *chakras* in eastern traditions):

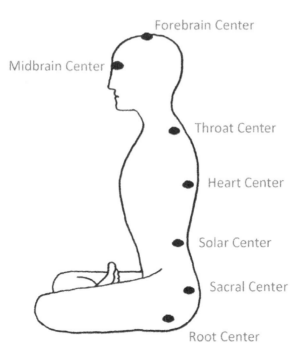

1. Assume your standard practicing posture.

2. Close your eyes and place your attention in the Root Center. Let it dwell there for about two minutes.

3. Now, move your attention to the Sacral Center and stay there for about two more minutes.

4. Do the same for the remaining five energy centers. See the illustration to know their placement. It should be done by paying attention to the inner sensations and vital force in each location.

This practice should take 14 minutes overall. In the initial stages, the practitioner is merely trying to get acquainted with the energy centers' presence. Once their presence is easily palpable, it is time to move into the next technique.

Technique #2

1. Place yourself in your standard meditative posture, relax, and breathe deeply and slowly for a couple of minutes.

2. Close your eyes and feel the vital force within you. You may feel tingling all over the body, goosebumps, shivering energy through the spinal cord, or any other of the many possible effects.

3. Visualize your spinal nerve as a fine tube running from the Root Center in the perineum upwards to the Forebrain Center.

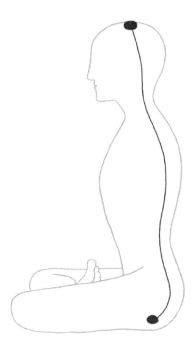

4. As you slowly inhale, trace the spinal nerve with your attention, going from the Root Center to the Forebrain Center. As you slowly exhale, trace it down from the Forebrain Center back to the Root Center.

This technique is quite similar to some pranayama techniques used by ancient yogis who had a similar objective of awakening the Secret Fire. There are other ways of awakening it, but this is one of the most efficacious.

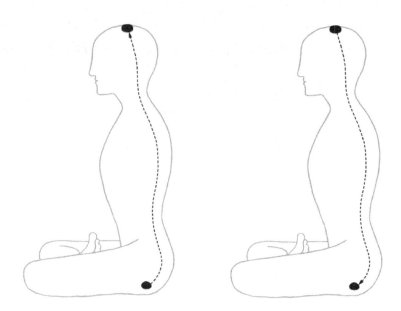

5. Repeat this process for anywhere between 10 to 90 minutes. Use a timer to track the duration of the practice. The more you do it, the better you'll get, and the deeper your experiences may become.

The breath's length is not significant; do it according to your current ability, but the slower and deeper your breathing is, the better.

Although initially you are visualizing and tracing the spinal nerve with your attention and slow breathing, given sufficient practice, you will begin to perceive the fine tube of the spinal cord.

Distractions will inevitably arise. If your attention diverts into other sensations or stimuli, go back to tracing the energy within your spinal nerve once you realize that you are off track.

This process can cause some inconveniences, such as feeling exhausted, tired, or dizzy, and it can even induce muscle spasms or bodily pain. Nonetheless, the student doesn't need to worry if any of these symptoms occur because they are transient and will eventually fade away a couple of hours after the practice ends. They may occur because the expansion and enhancement of our vital pathways and energy centers require a significant amount of energy, alertness, and focus. The mind and body will naturally need to draw the necessary energy from somewhere. The energy that would otherwise be applied to repairing the body, performing elaborate mental processes, digestion, and so on will be used for this practice.

Nevertheless, the student may also be free from any side effects. In actuality, practitioners of this technique often report feeling fresh, with a higher sense of vitality and more energy flowing through their body; in some instances, they detail the enhancement of sense perceptions and even the sudden emergence of mental abilities.

The Fire Method:

This method will not be the best for most students, but it's more powerful than the Yoke Method. Students should only attempt it if they have mystical or occult experience (i.e., it's not suitable for neophytes) and after having employed the previous method for a couple of months. Even though the results and experiences may be felt sooner with this method, it has the potential to generate more and stronger side-effects (e.g., headaches, dizziness, irascibility, impatience, etc.). It also requires diligence and devotion to the practice. Succinctly, it enhances everything from the previous method: you may perceive or experience more, but the unfavorable aftereffects may also be intensified.

Technique #1

1. Light seven candles around yourself in your laboratorium. These candles symbolize the seven energy centers within the spinal nerve where the Secret Fire will go through once awakened. In addition, they also emit heat, which will help with the practice. Then, sit in your standard posture, close your eyes, relax, and breathe deeply for a couple of minutes.

2. Visualize your spinal nerve as a fine tube running from the Root Center in the perineum to the Forebrain Center.

3. Feel the vital force electrifying the spine. You may feel tingling all over the body, goosebumps, shivering energy through the spinal cord, or any other of the many possible effects.

4. Visualize the Fire element symbol [Δ] at the Root Center. Try to feel as if it were emanating heat and energy.

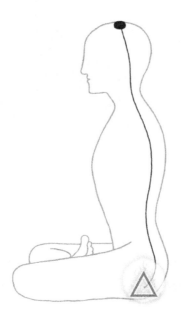

5. Inhale and hold the air.

6. Trace the spinal nerve with your attention, moving the Fire symbol from the Root Center to the Forebrain Center. Once your attention reaches the Forebrain Center, hold it there for two seconds, and then trace it down through the spinal nerve from the Forebrain Center back to the Root Center. Hold it in the Root Center for two seconds and repeat the whole movement.

Keep moving your attention up and down the spinal nerve with 2-second pauses at the top and bottom while holding your breath. The speed at which you trace the spinal nerve upwards and downwards is up to you, as long as you can feel as if a hot current of energy is moving through your spinal nerve.

7. Repeat this process for anywhere between 10 to 30 minutes. Use a timer to track the duration of the practice. The more you do it, the better you'll get, and the deeper your experiences may become. You may feel tingling all over your body, goosebumps, tremors of energy through your spinal cord, or any other of the many possible effects. It's a matter of time and sufficient practice until the fire erupts in complete ecstasy, steaming the entire body.

The Union Method:

This method should seldomly be attempted because it can easily lead the practitioner off the path. It involves employing sexual alchemy to awaken the Secret Fire by utilizing our sexual energy. This is achieved by preventing orgasm and channeling the build-up of sexual energy from the sacral region towards the brain. Instead of physically orgasming, the student continuously raises the energy through the spinal nerve until it reaches the brain with the aid of deep and slow breathing. If this action is done repeatedly, the gathered energy will be so intense that it will awaken the Secret Fire, giving the student a powerful mystical orgasm.

It's easy to be lost in the pleasures of sexual intercourse and fail to achieve the objective of this method. Therefore, it requires legitimate spiritual know-how and mystical maturity.

These three methods employ the use, control, generation, and restraint of vital force to awaken the Secret Fire. Various mystical experiences can occur during this practice, such as having visions, feeling like the body is floating, experiencing inner electric-like currents, or perceiving a rainbow of colors (indicative of the Secret Fire going through each energy center).

Sometimes, the student can feel sexual arousal during this practice, but that's nothing to worry about; it's a normal sign of progress that some practitioners experience, and it will pass after a while. Perspiration or feeling a tangible inner warmth is also a common effect. There are many possible temporary consequences to the physical body and mind (even fainting), but it's virtually impossible to point out what may exactly occur; there's no concrete scenario for what may or may not happen to the student internally and externally, because it's largely dependent on each student's conditioning, nervous system, and mental maturity.

The awakening of this powerful fire energy marks the opening of your inner gates into the Universe's greatest mysteries. Additionally, your perception and sensitivity of how reality operates will become enhanced, and the physical body's functioning and vitality will also improve. It's a spiritual and physical rebirth.

This marriage of the Secret Fire with the still consciousness marks the true conjunction of Mercury and Sulfur; in their coalescence, they become one as they've always been, reunited at last. The climax of this union is a coming back to one's origins, a union with the First Matter, though only as an experience. Admittedly, they aren't true opposites because, just like fire and warmth, they aren't separated.

The Great Work is not completed in this stage because the student fails to sustain and integrate this elated state into their body, energy, and mind. That's why some alchemists call it the "Lesser Stone." But despite being called "lesser", this is one of the most important steps in the alchemical path towards the Philosopher's Stone.

To maintain such power and create the Philosopher's Stone, the student needs to incubate and ground this divine experience and fire energy into themselves. It's there where we go next.

The Inner Furnace

After the potency of the previous practices, the student needs to "digest" the accumulated energy into their body and mind to embody Spirit and spiritualize the body. This digestion allows the energy to gently mature and expand within the body and mind (an inner alchemist's actual furnace). The assimilation of the newfound vitality, sagacity, and raw mystical power will also occur.

Once the student succeeds in connecting with the Secret Fire multiple times, they must create a token or conditioning that will instantly bring back that state of connection. The symbol used for this is Mercury.

Mercury is a powerful alchemical symbol and, among its many uses and meanings, symbolizes the awakened Secret Fire. Its similarity to the female symbol (♀) is no coincidence. It's often seen as "female energy", thus the similarity. The Secret Fire is universal energy in its dynamic form; it's the "movement" of God, the motion of everythingness, God-Force, as explained in chapter "Alchemical Trinity".

Every time you visualize this symbol with your mind, it should quickly invoke your connection with the Secret Fire, thereby altering your state of consciousness. This will only be possible if you've achieved the goal of the previous practice and become adept at it.

Every time you perform the Conjunction of Sulfur and Mercury and successfully awaken or connect with the Secret Fire (or even if you just briefly experience its splendor), you must try to visualize or, at least, think about the symbol of Mercury. You must create a connection between this token and the "experience" of the Secret Fire. This will require time and patience.

You can gauge your progress by sitting down in your laboratorium, visualizing this symbol in your mind, and trying to recollect the state of mind or being from the experience of the Secret Fire. The quicker and stronger it appears, the more powerful the Alchemical Distillation will be.

Once the desired state is present, you need to incubate this energy and state in your inner furnace, as if you were giving them a perfect environment to mature, develop, and integrate with your body and mind. Imagine that yellow-golden energy envelopes your body and mind as you let the energy and state integrate.

As a result of the awakening and rise of the Secret Fire, and as the digestion and integration of that energy and state become more deep-rooted within the student's consciousness, a permanent and conscious connection with the First Matter is created. This connection must be nurtured and crystallized; it is the way towards the Philosopher's Stone, mainly because the "essence" of the Philosopher's Stone is found in the First Matter.

This intimate connection with our core generates a powerful presence that emanates from within, overflowing every perception with a fresh delightfulness. Instead of practicing alchemy to transform into divinity or God, the divine or God now directly transmutes the student's psyche.

SECTION 4

The Alchemist

13

Alchemical Distillation

At this juncture, the student is no longer regarded as a student of alchemy but as an alchemist. Only alchemists can undergo this late phase of the alchemical path and complete the Great Work.

Previously, the alchemist united Mercury with Sulfur in the Above, and integrated that experience. The goal was the spiritualization of the mind, energy, and body. Now, the alchemist must welcome Sulfur to the Below and materialize Spirit. This is a prelude to the coagulation into the Philosopher's Stone.

Traditional distillation is the conversion of a liquid into vapor and the ensuing conversion of the vapor back to liquid form. However, in Inner Alchemy, it symbolizes the alchemist's ascension into the divine and descent of the divine into the material.

Alchemical distillation is not a singular process that a practitioner can employ but a set of alchemical procedures that has begun, unperceived by the alchemist, in earlier practices.

It ascends from Earth to Heaven, and again descends to Earth. And thereby gathers to Itself the powers of things Above, and of things Below.

— Hermes Trismegistus,
Tabula Smaragdina

The alchemist has already achieved the ascension from Earth to Heaven and the descent back to Earth. This was required to unlock a "channel" to the alchemist's divine essence to embody the "qualities" of Spirit or God. But to gather the powers of things Above and of things Below, and coagulate them into a new self, it is necessary to employ this final step of the distillation process.

The student began with a long process of purification, followed by the transmutation of the psyche. Subsequently, equipped with a more capable body, energy, and mind, the student merged the opposite forces within and transcended into Above. Afterwards, they brought the Above into Below, integrating it into all of their being. Now, the alchemist has to sublimate and refine the material and the spiritual within themselves, ensuring that no impurities or submerged shadow from the previous identity laying around in potentiality, within unconscious parts of the psyche, infiltrate into the manifestation of the new self on the coagulation process.

This is accomplished in two phases: first by performing the circulation of spiritual light with the seal of Sulfur, and finally, by letting the world, matter, and everything non-mystical inundate Spirit, as paradoxically as it may appear.

Phase I - Distillation of Liquid Light

1. Begin by trying to sense the divine presence within. Because of your long journey of alchemical purification and practice, feeling a divine presence within will be straightforward. It's a subtle yet palpable, joyful yet powerful presence that emanates from within and expands around your body. Let this divine presence consume you for about 10 to 20 minutes.

2. Visualize the symbol of Sulfur glowing within your heart. Feel the divine presence melt into the symbol of Sulfur. This symbol represents Spirit within you. With each naturally slow breath, it glows more and more.

3. Imagine liquid light transporting the divine presence coming out of the symbol of Sulfur, expanding through your whole nervous system.

4. Continue circulating the liquid light for 10 to 20 minutes.

This distillation of liquid light must be repeated for months until sufficient liquid light accumulates in the nervous system and crystallizes in the center of the brain. It will be experienced as seeing a powerful white and euphoric light when you close your eyes or sit to practice. Once this light begins to appear, you will intuitively know what to do; essentially, it's about observing it and being absorbed by it. It's an intimate process that varies by each alchemist.

Phase II – World Laboratorium

In the second phase, the alchemist has to go into the world and stop doing anything related to alchemy: let the matter inundate Spirit.

Everything the alchemist has done up to this point is to spiritualize the mind, energy, and body; to go beyond the matter into the divine was always the ambition. But leaving the Earth and flying through the heavens leaves the alchemist's mind with no ground to stand on when the hardships and difficulties of daily life arise. Regardless of living in a monastery or wide-open world of society, the universe will keep throwing challenges at those who are prepared to face them. And let's not deceive ourselves: perfection and spiritual growth are always a journey in progress despite the alchemist's level of progress. Divinity is not a light switch that is turned on but a constant and conscious will to allow the transcendental to gleam through our current vessel in whatever realm we currently are.

This may be the longest phase of the whole alchemical journey. Many have failed here because they forget about alchemy and their mystical expedition, and get swelled by what the ancient Vedic texts call "Maya", the illusion.

There are two probable conclusions to this phase (which lasts no less than a year):

- You get seduced by the ebb and flow of worldly pleasures; you lose track and become so mired with the world that alchemy is locked in a drawer deep inside your mind, never to be remembered again. Occasionally, it crops up in your thoughts, to which you respond: "One day, I will go back to practicing it and realize my divine potential. Just not right now!").

If this happened, then you've progressed too quickly and failed to thoroughly practice and experience each method and technique along the alchemical path. The mental states and energy you thought were fully integrated were only short-lived experiences.

The best course of action now is to go back to the beginning and progress from there. You will advance much faster due to the "muscle memory effect" that occurs with mystical practices and previously experienced mental states, but make sure you take your time and go unhurriedly.

- You have successfully engaged with the world, but you've continuously perceived and experienced it through the spiritual outlook of alchemy. Life is not the same as it used to be before this pilgrimage, and neither are you.

Before commencing the alchemical journey, the trials and tribulations of life would lead you to a dark place, overflowing you with beliefs, conditionings, traits, emotions, and habits that curbed your ability to fully experience life. However, this time was different: you were prepared.

All of the practices and multi-dimensional transmutations that you have gone through have given you the required maturity and experience to endure anything with integrity, peace, and wisdom; they have given you a divine presence, and that is now your guide. It is a real guide, and you can distinctly hear its silent voice, which is above and beyond all previous experiences of intuition. And if this is the case, you are ready to finalize the "becoming" of the Philosopher's Stone.

14

Becoming the
Philosopher's Stone

ncient literature is brimming with clues and approaches
on how to create the Philosopher's Stone. This process
is not something that is done once and is done forever,
but a journey that lasts many years or even lifetimes.

Some people read about alchemy and dream of gold,
wisdom, and unconceivable transmutations. However, the
majority of people look at it with indifference, affirming it
to be a pseudo-science of the past, relegated to the caliber
of a "fairy-tale." They hear that many ancient alchemists
achieved immortality as a result of their bizarre compounds,
created by dissecting dead species and by using substances

such as sulfur, mercury, and salt, amid other materials. But by now, we know that this type of alchemy will not truly transform us.

Notwithstanding the conflicting stories and opinions on alchemy, wouldn't it be wise to, at least, investigate some of these fables and discover whether they bear any truth at all?

Most people would run to the end of the world, suffering through any adversity if confronted with the possibility of finding gold or a few bright diamonds. These same people wouldn't put in one hour of their time searching for one of the greatest gold mines in the world: the Philosopher's Stone.

It is called a stone, but it is not a stone; it's not a chimerical dream, but an existing living reality, which can be attained by leaving the shores of nescience in the caravel of alchemy.

Alchemical Dragon

To finalize the creation of the Philosopher's Stone, the alchemist must reflect and contemplate the period spent during the second part of the Alchemical Distillation. Through this contemplation, countless understandings will surface, but there's one that will stand out above the rest: to achieve the ultimate alchemical success, it isn't only a matter of becoming divine but also of realizing the full potential of our humanity. The humanization of the immortal spirit and the divinization of the material body coagulate into a new self. This new, refined, and pure Salt (ego) must be recreated as a perfect "Divine Child" or "Philosopher's Child".

The mythical Phoenix is seen as the alchemical symbol of coagulation; the old self dies, and a new self is born. The resurrected self is the Divine Child, manifesting the new divine awareness beyond the alchemist's opposites. However, I have recognized on my own process that there's a more powerful symbol to represent this coagulation, which comes after the Phoenix: the *Ouroboros*.

While the Phoenix represents the death of the old self and the resurrection of a new illuminated self, the Ouroboros embodies the infinite flux of death and rebirth that every soul in Creation experiences; it represents both the infinite and the finite. The Ouroboros is a dragon eating its own tail; it's a powerful archetypal energy inherent to Creation, representing limitless energy, spiritual immortality, and God-Consciousness. The Ouroboros is essential to become the living Philosopher's Stone and achieve true immortality, and the alchemist will have to unleash it.

The Ouroboros encircles the synergy of the elements, creating the Philosopher's Stone.

Although an expression of the First Matter, which is present in all things and in itself being nothing, the alchemist's self is an ever-improving version of itself, becoming an ever-better manifestation of All That Is. Therefore, it is also represented in the Ouroboros.

To unleash the inner Ouroboros, the alchemist will have to use all of their might to go to the source, embrace the divine presence, and ask the sacred intuition that guided them through the second phase of Alchemical Distillation for the final transmutation. Only those who are pure enough will be able to invoke its power because it's not something that can be done or performed.

Once the alchemical dragon has been released, the only thing the alchemist can do is surrender. This surrendering is achieved by being still; being still with the body, energy, mind, and soul.

Being devoured by the dragon allows the alchemist to experience what cannot be described in words. Simply put, the alchemist achieves the apotheosis of alchemy. What ensues is up to each one to discover. The gold of perfection is now yours. Perhaps your soul will then decide whether to merge with All That Is at the end of this incarnation or embark on a new adventure with a particular purpose. Who knows? As the living Philosopher's Stone, only you will know.

15

Magnum Opus

Initially, it may seem as if the discipline of alchemy is inadequate and unqualified for those who desire to pursue enlightenment and higher mystical arts.

The mystification of its process certainly creates an impenetrable fog for those unequipped with the required tools of understanding. This barrier to entry, accompanied by an unpurified mind, energy, and body, deter most students from reaching the appropriate depth, never going past the initial phases. But to become a legitimate alchemist, you must acquire a masterful understanding of the nature of reality and of your own self.

Afterwards, you can use this knowledge to transform any

aspect you desire and even to change the world around you. You may even use the principles of alchemy in your everyday life in ways that you've never thought of before. If we allow it, alchemy becomes all-embracing in every dimension of our lives. After all, alchemy is not a "death thing"; it's very much alive, and evolving, though the goal of immortality remains.

In the alchemical quest for gold and for the elixir of life, the alchemist will discover immortality, not in the body but in the soul. The deathlessness of the soul is known once it unites with Spirit.

Inevitably, to achieve the Magnum Opus, every alchemist will have to go through the same phases of alchemy: first, swim in the blackness that pervades the mind with ignorance, fragility, and uneasiness, until they wake up to the inner light that paints the black canvas with bright white. As they awake to the light in the whiteness, the light becomes so incandescent that it turns yellow-golden, shining brightly until the alchemist becomes the living reddish Philosopher's Stone.

Contemporary alchemy may never transcend the brotherhoods of secret societies and occult initiations, but at least, those who discover and practice it through the guidance of works like this are better equipped to uncover its hidden brilliance; and there is much of it yet to be rediscovered. Times are changing, and so are each one of us.

Ultimately, whether The Great Work of Alchemy is a man-made creation, or the fruit of divine intervention is irrelevant. All humans are potentially divine, and alchemy makes that potential a reality. You can make it a reality.

Epilogue

Ancient alchemists used to say that once an aspirant plunges into the alchemical path, the required teachings and instructions begin to appear in their lives in one form or another. This work may mark the beginning of such a journey, and although it provides tools on how to explore the world of Inner Alchemy, this is just one of many doors you will open.

An alchemist must dedicate their whole life to fully understand the intricacies of alchemy and overcome harsh trials to realize its secrets. They must be willing to take on this journey without any material reward or praise from others. Most people are unable to embrace it for very long. They choose instead to seek short-term solutions that require little effort on their part but do not provide lasting change. But there is no prize without perseverance and fortitude.

If you are willing to commit to the alchemical practices and path, you will assuredly succeed in achieving the most beautiful and profound transmutations. Alchemy not only becomes a way of life but completely transforms it. I hope this work motivates you to go far into Inner Alchemy and achieve inner and outer success.

I wish you Godspeed.

Want to read more books like this? Show your feedback with a sincere review, or send an email to the author at mysticsarom@gmail.com, telling him what you thought about the book and what you'd like to see in new books (more mystic, occult and spiritual content, sharing more knowledge regarding practices, divine abilities, metaphysical explorations, etc.).

www.sacredmystery.org

Publications

The Art of Mysticism

The Step-by-step practical guide to Mysticism
& Spiritual Meditations

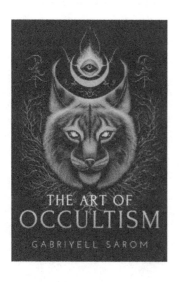

The Art of Occultism

The Secrets of High Occultism &
Inner Exploration

The Art of Magick

The Mystery of Deep Magick &
Divine Rituals

**Subscribe to Gabriyell Sarom's
Newsletter and receive the book:**

*Divine Abilities: 3 Techniques to Awaken
Divine Abilities*

www.sacredmystery.org

Made in the USA
Las Vegas, NV
12 October 2023

78912528R00083